M000196732

A Special Gift for

_____

from

_____

on

_____

Date

Visit Tyndale's exciting Web site at www.tyndale.com

Love Notes from God

By Mary Hollingsworth. Copyright © 2003 by Mary Hollingsworth , Shady Oaks Studio, 1507 Shirley Way, Bedford, Texas 76022. All rights reserved.

Artwork copyright © 2000 Artville, LLC.

Published by Tyndale House Publishers, Inc.

Research and writing associate: Vicki P. Graham

Series General Editor: Mary Hollingsworth

Published in Association with Educational Publishing Concepts, Wheaton, IL.

No portion of this material may be reproduced in any way whatsoever without the express written permission of the publisher.

ISBN 0-8423-7755-7

Printed in Canada.

03 04 05 06 07 08 — 6 5 4 3 2 1

Mary Hollingsworth's

Love Notes™

from GOD

Mary Hollingsworth's

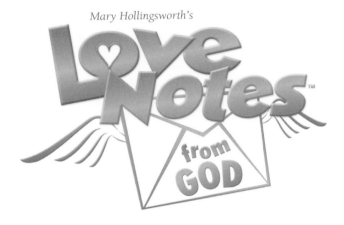

Love Notes™
from GOD

by
Mary Hollingsworth

Contents

Foreword . . . .*xii*

CHAPTER ONE

Love Notes from Heaven
I'll Hear You When You Call 1

CHAPTER TWO

The Invitation
I Love You for Making a Difference 15

CHAPTER THREE

The Tablecloth
I Love the Work You Do 29

CHAPTER FOUR

Fraidy Cat
I Love How You Care for Others 41

CHAPTER FIVE

A Voice from the Deep
I Will Help You in Times of Trouble 55

CHAPTER SIX

The Answer
I Will Answer Your Prayers 71

CHAPTER SEVEN

The Picture
I Will Lead You Home 91

Foreword

The love of God is immeasurable and sure. Nothing can destroy it. Nothing can weaken or break it. Nothing can deprive us of it. Nothing in all the world can take it from our hands, if we cling to it with all our hearts.

The love of God is enormous—bigger than the universe it created, as deep as his grace on the cross, as strong as his omnipotent power, as sweet as the song of the Shepherd, as refreshing as streams of eternal water in the desert, as warm as the holy fire that ignites our hearts.

God is the lover of our souls. And he sends us messages of his amazing love every day—love notes from heaven, as it were. These notes are delivered to us in unique and special ways, and each time the way a note comes is exactly the way it's needed. He sends fragrant, crimson roses to the gardens that we pass when our hearts are heavy. He hugs us with the arms of a loving family member. He comforts us with the words of a cherished friend. He gives us hope through the exuberant life of a child. And he infuses us with assurance through his precious Word.

Love Notes from God will bless you with the incredible love of God and will help you learn to look for his expressions of love in unexpected and delightful places. It will challenge you, too, to send love notes to the ones who grace your life and heart.

Mary Hollingsworth

Series General Editor

The love of God is greater far
than tongue or pen can ever tell;
It goes beyond the highest star,
and reaches to the lowest hell;
Oh, love of God, how rich and pure!
How marvelous and strong!
It shall forevermore endure—
the saints' and angels' song.

Could we with ink the ocean fill,
and were the skies of parchment made;
Were every stalk on earth a quill,
and ev'ry man a scribe by trade;
To write the love of God above
would drain the ocean dry;
Nor could the scroll contain the whole,
tho' stretched from sky to sky.

—F. M. Lehman, 1917

xiii

I know the plans I have for you—
plans to prosper you
and not to harm you,
plans to give you hope and
a future.

–Jeremiah 29:11, adapted

CHAPTER ONE

Love Notes from Heaven

I'll Hear You
When You Call

When Carolyn arrived at her office that morning, a cloud of impending doom seemed to have descended. People were standing in small, quiet clusters, whispering and shaking their heads.

Carolyn walked down the long hall to her office. Setting her partially consumed cup of McDonald's coffee on the desk, she noticed the official-looking memo from the owner of the publishing company in her in-box. The memo said that her division of the company was being sold to a large publishing corporation. She felt a huge knot tighten in her stomach, and she sank down slowly into her familiar chair as she continued to read.

The memo went on to say that she could choose

to continue working for her division in her current position as an editor . . . at the new company in a distant part of the metroplex. Or, she could remain with her current company in a less exciting position. Neither prospect seemed particularly inviting to Carolyn.

Now what, Lord? she thought wearily. *I've just gotten back on my feet. Do I have to start all over again? And if so, what should I do?*

Then a quiet thought stole softly into her mind: *Why don't you write?*

"Oh, that's ridiculous," she said aloud to herself. Then she looked around to make sure no one had heard. *I have no writing track record,* she thought. *No one knows me from a hole in the ground. That's just a nice dream. Oh sure, so I've had two gift books published. That's no big deal. No, I could never make it as a writer; my skills are just not that good.*

Carolyn shook her head, as if to shake that silly thought from her mind for good. She slid the memo into her desk drawer to think about later. Still, as the day wore on, the idea of writing niggled at the back of her mind. She wondered if, indeed, she might actually become a freelance writer. *It's risky. Uncertain. A silly idea,* she thought.

When Carolyn got home that night, her thoughts returned to the dilemma she faced. She decided, just for fun, to explore the idea of becoming a freelancer. What could it hurt? So she called a couple of writers she had often hired for projects and talked to them about the freelance life.

Encouraged somewhat by them, she went to her files and began dragging out manuscripts she had been writing in her spare time. Some were complete; others weren't. But the more she looked at the manuscripts, the more cautiously excited she became.

Some of these are OK, even pretty good, she thought

to herself. *Well, humility was never one of my strong suits.*

There were children's books, gift books, and ideas for nonfiction books. She also had a small binder that contained dozens of ideas for books she wanted to write sometime, as well as title ideas, character names, intriguing plot lines, and words and phrases she wanted to incorporate. *Maybe, just maybe, I could make it,* she thought to herself.

The next day, Carolyn went to see a fellow editor and friend. She showed her the manuscripts and asked if she thought they had any merit. The friend was enthusiastic about Carolyn's chances of getting them accepted and published.

"Come on, Carolyn, what have you got to lose?" she asked.

My shirt! thought Carolyn. "Well, thanks, for the vote of confidence."

Now Carolyn really had a dilemma on her hands. Should she, or shouldn't she? Could she make it financially, or would she go broke? Should she stay, or should she go out on her own? Her head was swimming with questions and anxieties.

She took her sack lunch and went to the park for some peace and quiet. But her thoughts were doing somersaults. Finally she put her lunch aside, turned her face toward heaven, and said, "Lord, please show me what you want me to do. I really want to do whatever you have planned for me, but I'm not sure if this is it, and I'm scared. Lord, you know that I'm not too bright about some things, and I don't understand subtleties. So, please, give me some kind of obvious sign that I can't possibly misunderstand that this is really what you want me to do. I need to know that it will work financially. I'll try to do whatever you want me to, Lord. I love you. Amen."

Then that same amazing thought seemed to dance

through her mind again: *Why don't you write?*

On October 31, 1988, Carolyn resigned her position with the company and, thirty minutes later, dropped ten manuscripts in the mail to different publishing companies. Within ten days she had sold all ten books.

On November 10 she looked up toward heaven from the last acceptance letter, laughing and crying at the same time, and shouted, "I've got it, Lord! I understand. Thank you!"

Carolyn has continued to write because she knows that those letters from the publishers were much more than mere acceptance letters for books; they were God's direction for her life. They were love notes from heaven.

A true story
with fictional names

At the touch of Love
everyone becomes a poet!

–Plato

The Old Refrain

Fritz Kreisler, the great violinist, found himself in Hamburg, Germany, one evening with an hour to spare before taking a boat to London, where he was to play the following evening. So he wandered into a music shop.

The proprietor asked to see Fritz's violin, which he carried under his arm. In a moment the proprietor disappeared, only to reappear with two policemen. One laid his hand on Kreisler's shoulder and said, "You are under arrest."

"For what?" asked Kreisler.

"You have Fritz Kreisler's violin."

"Well, I am Fritz Kreisler."

"Come, come," said the policeman, "you can't

pull that one on us. Come to the station."

Kreisler's boat sailed in an hour. He had to do some quick thinking. He looked around, and in the corner he saw a Victrola. Kreisler asked the proprietor if he had any of Fritz Kreisler's records. He produced "The Old Refrain," put it on the Victrola, and played it through.

"Now," Kreisler said, "please let me have my violin." Then, with all the skill he could command, he played "The Old Refrain." When Kreisler was through, he asked, "Are you satisfied now?"

With profuse apologies, they bowed him out of the shop to freedom.

Sometimes, even when God sends us expressions of his love, we can't believe it, or perhaps we just don't recognize them. We are often looking for his love to swoop in on giant eagle's wings when, in reality, it most often floats in on the soft, gossamer wings of butterflies.

A   True   Story

A Love Note from God

Listen to me. . . . I have
cared for you since before
you were born.

–Isaiah 46:3, adapted

Your Love Note to God

Dear God,

_____

_____

_____

_____

_____

_____

_____

_____

I love you. _____

I love you, I love you!
With a love that will not die
Till the sun grows cold,
And the stars are old,
And the leaves of the
Judgment Book unfold!

—Bayard Taylor

*I*nvest what you have
in others,
because after a while
you will get a return.

———————————

–Ecclesiastes 11:1, adapted

CHAPTER TWO

The Invitation

I Love You for
Making a Difference

$\mathcal{S}$he was no ordinary music teacher. Jessica Davis, or "Ms. D" as the kids called her, cared . . . really cared about her students at Central Junior High School where she had taught for so many years. She was more than their teacher—she was a friend, a mentor, a nurse, a counselor, and, when necessary, a fill-in mother.

Still, after twenty-six years in the classroom, what do I have to show for it? she wondered. *Tired feet. A closet full of trinkets and apple mementos. A shelf full of school annuals. And a measly retirement fund that I can't possibly live on.*

The longer she thought about it, the more she was convinced that it was time to move on. She needed to do something else with the rest of her life—something more lucrative, something where she could get the recognition she deserved, something fun, something that didn't smell like chalk dust and school cafeteria food.

She glanced down at the unsigned contract on her desk. Did she really want to sign up for yet another year of junior high kids with overactive hormones, zits, and squirmy bodies? Giggling girls who couldn't match pitch and boys whose voices were squeaking and changing?

Jessica sighed as she got up from her desk and went to her small kitchen to make a cup of her favorite raspberry tea. She always thought more clearly with a cup of tea. As she waited for the kettle to begin its song, she stared out her kitchen window. In the park across the street she saw a yellow kite with a homemade tail floating on the spring breeze. Higher and higher it rose. *That's what I want to do*, thought Jessica. *I want to fly! I don't want to be tied down anymore. I want to do what I want, when I want, where I want.*

Dropping the wet teabag into the trash, she took her cup of tea and walked resolutely back to her desk. She opened her desk drawer and took out a sheet of classic beige stationery, then picked up her favorite old Sheaffer fountain pen and began to write her letter of resignation to the school board.

Half an hour later, after carefully wording the letter, she folded it inside the unsigned contract and put it in the business-size envelope she had addressed in her best penmanship.

Am I doing the right thing, Lord? she wondered mentally. She sat for several minutes holding the envelope in her hand, staring at the washable blue ink, pondering the impact her letter would have on her life and others'. At last she rose and went to the front door. As she opened the door, she saw the postman just leaving her mailbox in his white-red-and-blue truck. She had just missed him. *Oh well, tomorrow will be soon enough,* she thought to herself.

Opening the mailbox to put her letter inside, she found a classy-looking, embossed envelope addressed to "Ms. D." She took it out and put her resignation letter in its place, raising the little red flag on the side of the mailbox. As she turned the expensive envelope over to examine it, she strolled back toward the house.

The spring air was warm and wonderful, and the gentle breeze kissed her cheeks and made her smile. So she sat down in her old oak porch swing and carefully opened the letter. Pushing the swing back and forth, back and forth with one toe, she began to read:

Dear Ms. D,

You may not remember me, but I was one of your students at Central Junior High School about ten years ago. You might remember me by the nickname the other kids called me: Frumpy.

Frumpy! Sure, she remembered—an overweight girl with stringy hair and terrible skin; from a poor family, homemade clothes. . . . But, oh yes, an unusual musical gift. A big, rich voice and the talent to sing with feeling and interpretation. She returned to the letter with more interest.

I'm writing to say thank you . . . for so many things. Thank you for believing in me when no one else did. Thank you for helping me see past my acne-covered face to my real potential. Thank you for caring enough to spend extra time with me after school giving me private voice lessons . . . for free. Thank you for seeing beyond Frumpy to fine.

The enclosed documents are my small way of showing my appreciation for all you did for me, whether you knew it or not. It would mean so much to me if you accept.

Blessings and thanks,

Jerilyn Russeau

Setting the letter aside, Jessica picked up the envelope again with curiosity. Inside she found a round-trip airline ticket to New York City and an engraved invitation on cream-colored parchment paper. The raised, gold lettering bespoke its expense and importance.

Carnegie Hall cordially invites you
to attend the debut performance of
Miss Jerilyn Russeau,
soprano, with the
New York Philharmonic Orchestra
on Saturday evening,
the twelfth of June
at eight o'clock in the evening.

Smiling with heart-bursting pride, she read the invitation again. *Frumpy at Carnegie Hall. Wow! And she thinks I helped her get there in some small way.*

As warm tears spilled out of her eyes and down her cheeks, Jessica pushed her toe down to stop the squeaking swing. She paused for several seconds, thinking. Then, getting up, she walked slowly off the porch and out to the mailbox, put the red flag down, and removed the beige letter. Turning back to the house, she glanced up and smiled at the cloudless sky.

Thank you, Lord. I got your letter.

Let no man shrink
from the bitter tonics
Of grief, and yearning,
and need, and strife,
For the rarest chords
in the soul's harmonies
Are found in the minor
strains of life.

———

–Ella Wheeler Wilcox

Give It Away

On opening night of *South Pacific* on Broadway, musical star Mary Martin was handed a note as she was ready to go on stage. The note was handwritten from Oscar Hammerstein, who Mary knew was lying on his deathbed. The note said simply:

> Dear Mary,
> A bell's not a bell till you ring it. A song's not a song till you sing it. Love in your heart is not put there to stay. Love isn't love till you give it away.

It's a wonderful concept, isn't it? God was love itself from before time began, but we only knew of his love when he knelt down and gave it to us in a gift hung on a tree for us. People around us come to know his love only when we reflect and refract that love into the dark corners of this lonely world. It is our joy to be notes of his love to others.

A Love Note from God

I will not forget the work you did
and the love you showed for
me by helping my people.
I want you to go on with the
same hard work all your life,
and you will surely get what
you hope for.

–Hebrews 6:10-11, adapted

Your Love Note to God

Dear God,

_____

_____

_____

_____

_____

_____

_____

I love you. _____

How precious are the
promises of God!
How wondrous is his Word!
How glorious is his saving grace!
How majestic is his hope!
How beautiful are the flowers
in his garden!
And how my heart aches with
love for him!

—Mary Hollingsworth

I had your mother give
birth to you.
I caused you to trust me
from the time you
were a baby.
So lean on me now
when trouble is near.
I won't be far away
and I will help you.

———

—Psalm 22:9–11, adapted

CHAPTER THREE

The Tablecloth

I Love the
Work You Do

*T*he brand new minister and his wife, newly arrived to reopen a church building in suburban Brooklyn, were excited about their opportunities. The church building, though it was very run-down, needed much work.

They set a goal to have everything done in time to have their first service on Christmas Eve. They worked hard, repairing pews, plastering walls, and painting, and on December 18 they were ahead of schedule and almost finished.

On December 19 a terrible tempest—a driving rainstorm—hit the area and lasted for two days. On the 21st, the minister went over to the church. His heart sank when he saw that the roof had leaked, causing a large area of plaster about twelve feet high by eight feet wide to fall off the front wall just behind the pulpit.

The minister cleaned up the mess on the floor, and not knowing what else to do but postpone the

Christmas Eve service, headed home. On the way he noticed that a local business was having a flea market sale for charity, so he stopped in.

One of the items for sale was a beautiful, hand-made, ivory-colored, crocheted tablecloth with exquisite work, fine colors, and the cross embroidered right in the center. It was just the right size to cover up the hole in the front wall. He bought it and headed back to the church.

By this time it had started to snow. An older woman, running from the opposite direction, was trying to catch the bus. She missed it. So the minister invited her to wait in the warm church for the next bus forty-five minutes later.

She sat in a pew and paid no attention to the minister while he got a ladder and hangers to put up the tablecloth as a wall tapestry. The minister could hardly believe how beautiful it looked, and it covered up the entire problem area.

Then he noticed the woman walking down the center aisle. Her face was pale—white like a sheet.

"Sir," she asked, "where did you get that tablecloth?"

The minister explained. Then the woman asked him to check the lower right corner to see if the initials E.B.G. were crocheted into it. They were— her initials, the woman who had made that tablecloth thirty-five years before in Austria.

The stunned woman explained to the minister that before the war she and her husband had been well-to-do people in Austria. When the Nazis came, she was forced to leave. Her husband was going to follow her the next week. She was captured, sent to prison, and never saw her husband or her home again.

The minister wanted to give her the tablecloth, but she made him keep it for the church. The minister insisted on driving her home; that was the least he felt he could do. She lived on the other side of Staten Island and was only in Brooklyn for the day for a housecleaning job.

What a wonderful service they had in the renovated church on Christmas Eve. The church was almost full. The music and the spirit were great.

At the end of the service, the minister and his wife greeted everyone at the door, and many said they would return. One older man, whom the minister recognized from the neighborhood, continued to sit in one of the pews and stare. The minister wondered why he   wasn't leaving.

The man asked him where he had gotten the tablecloth on the front wall, because it was identical to one that his wife had made years ago when they lived in Austria before the war. How could there be two tablecloths so much alike?

He told the minister how the Nazis came, how he forced his wife to flee for her safety, and how he was supposed to follow her. But he was arrested and put into a prison. He never saw his wife or his home again.

The minister asked the man if he would allow him to take him for a little ride. They drove to Staten Island to the same house where the minister had taken the woman three days earlier. He helped the man climb the three flights of stairs to the woman's apartment, and he knocked on the door. There he witnessed the greatest Christmas reunion he could ever imagine.

A true story as told
by Rob Reid

33

Love is a fabric
which never fades,
no matter how
often it is washed in
the waters of adversity
and grief.

—Anonymous

For Love and Roses

Comedian Jack Benny, while being one of the
funniest actors in our recent history, also had a
tender, loving side. He was completely in love
with his wife, who stayed by his side for decades,
through tough times and terrific times.

When Jack finally "arrived" as a recognized
and sought-after comedian, and his financial sta-
tus soared accordingly, he began sending his
lovely wife a single, long-stemmed, red rose
every day to thank her for her loyalty and to
express his undying love.

This practice went on for many years. Every
single day of every week of every year, the
beautiful rose arrived faithfully at the door of
their home. Even when Jack was out of town or
overseas, the roses kept coming, reminding her of

his never-failing love and devotion.

When Jack eventually died, his lifelong partner grieved bitterly, as would be expected. Unexpectedly, however, the single red rose continued to be delivered to her every day for over a week after the funeral. Finally, although it seemed so unlikely, she decided the florist was not aware of her husband's death. So she called to inform them that the roses probably should not be sent anymore.

To her sweet surprise, the florist said, "Oh no, Mrs. Benny. Your husband set up a special fund before he died to keep the roses coming to you every day for as long as you live. He wanted you to know that his love was, indeed, undying."

Such is the nature of true love. If we are careful to send tokens of our love to others while we live, our love will live on as beautiful roses in their memories long after we have gone.

A Love Note from God

I am the Lord, and I have heard
your prayer for help.
I am your strength and shield.
Trust me, and I will help you.
I am happy when you are happy;
I love your songs of praise.

–Psalm 28:6-7, adapted

Your Love Note to God

Dear God,

_____

_____

_____

_____

_____

_____

_____

_____

I love you. _____

How Fair the Rose

How fair is the Rose!

What a beautiful flower.

The glory of April and May!

But the leaves are beginning to

fade in an hour,

And they wither and die in a day.

Yet the Rose has one powerful

virtue to boast,

Above all the flowers of the field;

When its leaves are all dead,

and fine colors are lost,

Still how sweet a perfume

it will yield!

—Isaac Watts

I will make everything
possible for you if
you believe.

———————————

—Mark 9:23, adapted

CHAPTER FOUR

Fraidy Cat

I Love How You Care for Others

We got her at the place for friendless or abandoned animals. A tiny gray-and-white kitten whose eyes were still blue—just an alley cat, nameless, homeless, too young to lap milk from a saucer. We had to feed her with an eyedropper. She didn't like the strange new world in which she found herself. She hid under the bed and cried. We laughed and called her Fraidy Cat.

She soon got used to us, of course. She slept a lot and played games with balls of wadded paper. I never saw her chase her tail, as kittens are supposed to do. But she had a good time.

She had an even better time when we moved to the country. She was half-grown then and liked to stalk things in the tall grass behind the house. Twice she brought home a mouse for us to admire, and once a bird. Fortunately the bird wasn't hurt, so we took it away from her and let it go. She seemed to think our distinction between mice and birds was pretty silly. Logically, she was right.

She was an aloof little beast in those days—I say "little" because she remained a very small cat. She didn't show much affection for anyone. In fact, if you tried to pet her when she wasn't in the mood, she would dig her claws in harder than was pleasant, or even bite. This didn't bother me, of course, because I am really a dog man. I can take cats or leave them alone.

We acquired a dog soon after we moved to the country, a friendly boxer named Major. Fraidy loathed him. For the first month or so, if he came too close, she would spit and rake his nose, leaving him hurt and bewildered. I was rather indignant about this. After all, I'm a dog man. I slapped Fraidy once or twice for assaulting Major. "Who do you think you are?" I asked her. "Try to remember you're nothing but a cat!"

While she was still too young, in our opinion, for such goings-on, Fraidy decided to become a mother. When the time came, however, she didn't hide away like most cats. She stuck close to us. Maybe she had a hunch it was going to be tough. It was. There was only a single kitten, much too big. She couldn't handle it herself; I had to help her. It took all my strength, and I thought she would bite me, but she didn't. She just watched me, her yellow eyes glassy with pain. Afterwards, she licked my hand. But the kitten was born dead.

"Never mind, Fraidy," we said. "You'll have better luck next time."

For days she was gaunt and thin; she looked for the kitten everywhere. I believe she thought Major was responsible for its disappearance—all her old distrust of him came back, for a while. She got over that, but one thing she didn't get over: her gratitude to me. She followed me from room to room, and if I sat down she would jump into my lap, put her forefeet on my chest, and stare into my face with the most soulful look imaginable.

"Typical woman," my wife said, laughing. "In love with her obstetrician."

"It's just misplaced maternal instinct," I said. "She'll get over it as soon as she has some kittens."

Nature, it seemed, had the same idea, because before very long Fraidy was pregnant again. We figured she would have at least two kittens this time. Smaller ones. We were very happy for her. She seemed sleepy and satisfied.

Then one day, not long ago, she developed a cough. We thought nothing of it because her appetite was good. She seemed somewhat lethargic, but after all, her time was almost due. Then, early yesterday morning, she came up from the kitchen where she slept and jumped on our bed. She curled up in my lap and looked at me. She meowed unhappily.

"What's the matter with this fool cat?" I said. "What's she trying to tell us?"

All yesterday she didn't eat. She even refused water. In the evening, finally, I called a vet. There are good vets, I guess, and bad ones. This one—when he saw her—said it seemed to be just a cold. No fever. Nothing very wrong. That was yesterday.

This morning Fraidy Cat dragged herself upstairs again, but this time she couldn't jump onto the bed. She was too weak. The roof of her mouth was very pale; her eyes were glazed.

I telephoned another vet. It was Sunday morning, and early, but he said to bring her over. I did. He examined her carefully. He knew his business. You can always tell.

"I'm sorry," he said. "Uterine infection. I'm afraid the kittens are dead."

"Can't you operate?" I said. "Can't you save her?"

He shook his head. "I could try. But it would just

prolong things. She's pretty far gone now." He looked at my face. He was a kind man, and he loved animals. "I'd put her away," he said gently, "if I were you."

After a while I nodded my head.

"Now?" said the vet. "Or after you've gone?"

"I'll stay with her," I said.

He brought the hypodermic needle. "It doesn't hurt," he said. "She'll go to sleep, that's all." The needle went home, quick and merciful.

She was just an ordinary alley cat. She had no pedigree, no clever tricks. But I remembered how she'd roll over on the path when we'd drive up in the car. I remembered how she loved to eat slivers of melon from our breakfast plates. I remembered how she liked to have her ears scratched, and how she licked my hand the day I had to hurt her so terribly, the day her kitten was born dead.

I stood there with my hand touching her so that perhaps she would not be afraid. "It's all right,

Fraidy," I said. "Go to sleep. Go to sleep." And at last she put her head down on her clean little paws and closed her eyes.

I felt blindly for my pocketbook. It wasn't there. "I haven't any money," I said. "I'll have to send it to you."

"That's all right," the vet said. "Don't bother."

I touched her ear for the last time and turned back to the door. It was a golden summer morning, calm, serene. Down in the meadow a gigantic willow tree made a burst of greenness against the sky.

I got in the car quickly and drove away. But not far down the road I stopped the car and put my forehead against the steering wheel and wept. Because she was such a little cat. Because she had tried to tell me that she was sick, that she was in trouble, and I hadn't helped her. Not until too late. And I felt the awful emptiness that comes from not knowing how much you love something until you have lost it.

The way to love anything
is to realize that it might be lost.

—G. K. Chesterton

Really Real

"What is real?" asked the Rabbit one day, when they were lying side by side near the nursery fender, before Nana came to tidy the room. "Does it mean having things that buzz inside you and a stick-out handle?"

"Real isn't how you are made," said the Skin Horse. "It's a thing that happens to you."

"Does it hurt?" asked the Rabbit.

"Sometimes," said the Skin Horse, for he was always truthful. "When you are Real, you don't mind being hurt."

"Does it happen all at once?" he asked.

"It doesn't happen all at once," said the Skin Horse. "You become. It takes a long time. That's why it doesn't often happen to people who break easily, or have sharp edges, or who have to be carefully kept. Generally, by the time you are Real, most of your hair has been loved off, and your eyes drop out, and you get loose in the joints and very shabby. But these things don't matter at all, because once you are Real you can't be ugly, except to people who don't understand."

Margery Williams, *The Velveteen Rabbit*

A Love Note from God

I am love.
If you live in love, you live in me,
and I live in you.
There is no fear in love,
but perfect love drives your
fear away.

—1 John 4:16, 18, adapted

Your Love Note to God

Dear God,

_____

_____

_____

_____

_____

_____

_____

_____

I love you. _____

Love All

Love all God's creation,
the whole and every
grain of sand in it.
Love every leaf,
every ray of God's light.
Love the animals,
love the plants,
love everything.

If you love everything,
you will perceive the divine
mystery in things.
Once you perceive it,
you will begin to comprehend
it better every day.
And you will come at last
to love the whole world
with an all-embracing love.

—Fyodor Dostoyevsky

You may be sitting in darkness,
but I will be a light for you.

—Micah 7:8, adapted

CHAPTER FIVE

A Voice from the Deep

I Will Help You in Times of Trouble

We should have stopped sailing when we originally planned. But it was so easy to forget our worries on the sparkling Pacific, and we both needed an afternoon's escape.

Pepperdine University had been going through some difficult times. We had recently opened our new Malibu Beach campus, and we had kept our old one going in Los Angeles near the Watts area. Now we were beginning to wonder if we could operate both successfully. We had money problems, administrative problems, problems everywhere. So I was glad when my friend, Bill

Banowsky, our university president, suggested we take out the fourteen-foot catamaran.

Near sunset we came back to shore, beached the catamaran, and returned to our driftwood fire. Over the darkening Pacific, the wind was picking up. Bill looked at me with a glint in his eyes, and I knew what he had in mind.

"Great!" I said. "One more time."

Together we began to push the light craft down the sand toward the water. The catamaran is a cat-rigged sailboat composed of two long metal pontoons, which support a raised deck of canvas capable of holding two or three people. Because of its unique design, the craft slices through the water with exceptional speed and power.

As we slid the boat into the water, I was pushing on the starboard side, and Bill was standing at the stern. The surf foamed at our waists, and we prepared to hoist ourselves onto the canvas deck.

Suddenly the wind caught the sail and snapped it with the sound of a rifle crack. The boat shot forward like a bullet. I managed to grab the stern of the starboard pontoon and was instantly yanked off my feet. I found myself being dragged out to sea.

Bill lunged forward, trying to catch the boat, but he was left behind. The last I saw of him was his shocked face as he screamed, "Climb on!" But as the craft surged out to sea, I felt as if I were being dragged behind a runaway locomotive. I unsuccessfully tried to climb on board. Now it was too late to let go because the distance to shore was far greater than my swimming endurance.

As I was dragged along, the powerful water pressure pulled my pants off right over my shoes. I hung on, arms stretched before me, trying to keep my head above water. The ocean was icy, and my body was fast becoming numb.

I tried to pull myself up on the pontoon, but

try as I might, I couldn't lift myself even six inches. The racing water held me down and back. Panic filled me. This mindless craft would race on endlessly, towing me like some infuriated whale.

I tried to climb onto the pontoon again but fell back gasping. My arms were weakening; pain shot through my elbows and shoulders. How long could I hang on?

Alone under the darkening sky with only the roar of foaming water in my ears, I knew I faced death. *How ironic*, I thought, *when only minutes before I was warming myself contentedly by the beach fire and discussing the university's problems with Bill.*

My thoughts turned to Helen and our four children.

"Oh, God, help me, help me!" I gasped.

"Give me strength
to hang on."

My arms were like wood. I couldn't feel through my hands any more. *Once more. Just once more.* I called on my last remaining strength and threw a leg over the pontoon. Pain seared through me as the back of my knee struck a sharp metal projection, and blood ran down my leg. I slipped back deeper into the churning water, coughing and choking.

I was now at least two miles from shore. Even if a search was sent out, I despaired of anyone finding me in that vast ocean. Soon my hands would slip from the cold metal pontoon, and I would sink into the ocean depths, like a sailor buried at sea.

Now the waves increased in size, and I lost all hope as the cold, foaming breakers crashed down on me. So many times, as a minister, I had told others that "God is our protection and our

strength. He always helps in times of trouble"
(Psalm 46:1), but now my faith was weak, and I
was terrified.

Oh, God, help me, help me, I continued praying
as the surging catamaran pitched in the rolling
waves. Over and over those words flooded my
heart.

Then, as if prompted by something deep within me, my panicky feeling suddenly evaporated,
leaving me able to study my enemy, the ocean
waves. Until now, I had not been able to conquer
my fear long enough to really look at how to
combat the water. I saw now that each time the
bow of the catamaran rose to meet a big wave,
my end of the pontoon was momentarily buried
in the water.

I awaited my opportunity. Here came another
wave . . . there! I had managed to hoist my leg
over the pontoon.

Now wait. Here came another green, crashing

roller. Quick, lift!

By using the waves, I was able to shift more of my body out of the water. With each wave I was able to get more of me onto the pontoon. To my spent energy, God had added his power. Finally I lay on top of the boat's surface, hugging the cold metal, breathing hard. I looked up. The twenty-five-mile-per-hour wind was still driving us out to sea. It would be impossible to crawl forward to the tiller, but I could reach the rod guiding the rudder!

I shoved it as hard as I could, forcing the craft to turn toward shore. As she came about, the wind caught the sail with such enormous force that the boat capsized. But at least she was now dead in the water. I rolled onto the flat side of the exposed pontoon and lay there exhausted. "Thank you, God," I kept saying with every breath. "Thank you! Thank you!"

Then I heard it—a faint voice calling to me

out of the deep, out of the terrifying darkness. "Hang on, brother! Hang on!" *Was it the voice of God? And then I knew: Yes! It is God's voice calling to me through my friend.*

Bill and his son had commandeered a neighbor's boat and had come out to rescue me. I lay on the deck as we returned to shore; I was shivering cold, but my heart was singing songs of praise.

Love lifted me!
Love lifted me!
When nothing else
could help,
Love lifted me!

———————

James Rowe, 1912

Is Your Hut Burning?

The only survivor of a shipwreck was washed up on a small, uninhabited island. He prayed feverishly for God to rescue him, and every day he scanned the horizon for help, but none seemed forthcoming. Exhausted, he eventually managed to build a little hut out of driftwood for protection from the elements and to store his few possessions.

But then one day, after scavenging for food, he arrived home to find his little hut in flames, the smoke rolling up to the sky. The worst had happened; everything was lost.

He was stunned with grief and anger.

"God, how could you do this to me?" he cried.

Early the next day, however, he was awakened by the sound of a ship that was approaching the island. It had come to rescue him.

"How did you know I was here?" the weary man asked his rescuers.

"We saw your smoke signal," they replied.

It's easy to get discouraged when things are going badly. But we shouldn't lose heart, because God is at work in our lives, even in the midst of pain and suffering. Remember, next time your little hut is burning to the ground, it just may be a smoke signal that summons the grace of God.

A Love Note from God

Before you call, I will answer,
and I will help you while you
are still asking for help!

—Isaiah 65:24, adapted

Your Love Note to God

Dear God,

_____

_____

_____

_____

_____

_____

_____

_____

I love you. _____

The Love of God

The amazing, incredible,

overwhelming,

miraculous love of God,

through our nearsighted and

limited eyes,

is almost too good to be true—

almost, but not quite.

—Mary Hollingsworth

Ask, and I will give to you.
Search, and I will
help you find.
Knock, and I will open
the door for you.

—Matthew 7:7, adapted

CHAPTER SIX

The Answer

I Will Answer
Your Prayers

Jerri wiped her eyes for the hundredth time as she drove down Interstate 35 from North Dakota to Texas. She'd had a lot of time to think in the fifteen hours she had been on the road. Life had not turned out the way it was supposed to. Her husband, deciding he didn't want to be married anymore, had taken his clothes and left. She had found the infamous "Dear Jane" letter on the kitchen table when she came home.

Dear Jerri,

This is probably the biggest mistake I've ever made—I seem to

72

be good at that—but I just can't look at the hurt expression in your eyes anymore. I know I've let you down and treated you badly, and I don't want to keep doing it, but I don't seem to be able to stop.

So, I'm leaving. I need to spend some time alone to get my head back on straight. I hope you can understand and give me some time.

I love you. I will always love you, no matter what. Please forgive me.

Sam

That was two months ago. Sam had never come back. Never called. Never written. Never offered an additional explanation for his sudden departure. Jerri had no idea where he was.

So here she was, alone, headed south, back to Dallas where she had grown up. The huge old Chrysler was crammed to the windows with her clothes, personal files, linens, and other household items to help her set up an apartment back where she'd started ten years earlier.

Sure, she thought, *I have sheets and pillow cases. Just no bed! I have dishes, but no table to put them on or chairs to sit in. No appliances. No comfortable recliner. No end tables. No lamps. No sofa. And no money!*

"Lord," she said aloud, "please send me a sofa. Amen." And that quick, one-sentence prayer suddenly made her smile at herself. What a silly prayer. She laughed at herself silently.

At that moment she saw the exit to Euless, Texas (or "Useless" as many of the locals called it). So she concentrated on finding the apartment complex she had found on the

Internet. She thought she would like it and could afford it on the salary from her new job with the law firm.

After checking in at the main office, she was escorted to her new one-bedroom, unfurnished apartment. *Unfurnished,* she sighed. *Oh well, maybe God really will send me a sofa. Who knows?*

On Sunday she went to her old church and ran into a couple of her college friends. They introduced her to several other "suddenly singles" and took her to lunch to make her feel welcome. She felt quite cheered up after that and spent the afternoon moving her things from the car into the apartment.

About three o'clock the phone rang.

"Jerri, this is Carol. Listen, I'm getting some new living room furniture and wondered if you'd like to have my old sofa, just until you can get one you'd really like."

"I'd love it!" laughed Jerri. "You're a life saver."

"Great! My brother's coming over in his pickup, and we'll bring it to you in about an hour. OK?"

"Sure! That's great. And thanks, Carol."

And thanks, God, she thought after hanging up. *You're amazing!*

"Ask and you shall receive," she told herself.

About a week later Jerri and her friend Shannon were talking about their long-term plans to each buy a house. The biggest problem was coming up with the down payment, they agreed.

"I've got it!" said Jerri. "Why don't we share an apartment for a few months to save our money?"

"That's a great idea!" said Shannon excitedly. "And since you don't really have much furniture anyway, and I have lots, it will work out perfectly."

As they were moving Shannon into Jerri's apartment a couple of weeks later, Jerri had to smile when she noticed that Shannon had both a long sofa and a matching loveseat.

Thanks, Lord, she grinned. *I see you're still answering my prayer.*

The three sofas made a nice horseshoe-shaped conversation area in their living room. It was actually quite handy, and it didn't look half bad. Besides, it was only a temporary arrangement.

About three days later, Jerri met her friend Barbara for dinner. As dinner concluded Jerri said, "I'm glad you called, Barbara. It's really great to see you again."

"Well, before we leave, I have to confess that I had an ulterior motive," said Barbara. "I was talking to Carol yesterday, and she told me you didn't have a lot of furniture yet."

"Oh, well . . . " Jerri began to explain how things had changed since she'd seen Carol.

"Now, just let me finish," interrupted Barbara. "You see, my brother and his wife have purchased a new sofa and loveseat, but they need a place to store them for a few weeks until their house is finished. And I was hoping you might keep them until my brother's ready for them, since you have plenty of room."

"Uh, well, I don't really . . . "

"Yes, now, no arguments. You'll take the sofas and enjoy them until Rob can pick them up. He'll bring them over tonight. Gotta run. See ya!"

"But . . . but . . ." Jerri stammered as she watched Barbara leave.

Suddenly Jerri started laughing. She laughed so hard she cried. She knew now that everything in her life would turn out all right. All she had to do was ask.

Lord, thank you, thank you, and thank you. Next time I'll be more specific when I pray. And, oh yes, could you please stop sending me sofas now? I just don't know where I would put another one. I love you . . . more than I can ever say. Amen.

A true story

god loves and cares for
each one of us
as if there were only
one of us.

Augustine

Before You Ask

Helen Roseveare,
medical-missionary from England to Zaire, Africa

One night I had worked hard to help a mother in the labor ward but, in spite of all we could do, she died, leaving us with a tiny, premature baby and a crying two-year-old daughter. We would have difficulty keeping the baby alive as we had no incubator (since we had no electricity) and no special feeding facilities. Although we lived on the equator, nights were often chilly with treacherous drafts. One student midwife went to get the box we had for such babies and the cotton wool in which the baby would be wrapped.

Another student went to stoke up the fire and fill a hot-water bottle. She came back shortly in distress to tell me that as she filled the bottle it had burst. Rubber perishes easily in tropical climates. "And it is our last water bottle!" she exclaimed.

As in the West, it is no good crying over spilt milk, so in Central Africa it might be considered no good crying over burst water bottles. They do not grow on trees, and there are no drugstores down forest pathways.

"All right," I said. "Put the baby as near the fire as you safely can, and sleep between the baby and the door to keep it free from drafts. Your job is to keep the baby warm."

The following noon, as I did most days, I went to have prayers with the orphanage children. I gave the youngsters various suggestions of things to pray about and told them about the tiny baby. I explained our problem about keeping the baby warm enough, mentioning the hot-water bottle.

The baby so easily could die if it got chills. I also told them of the two-year-old sister, crying because her mother had died.

During the prayer time, one ten-year-old girl, Ruth, prayed the usual blunt prayer of our African children. "Please, God," she prayed, "send us a water bottle. It'll be no good tomorrow, God, as the baby will be dead, so please send it this afternoon."

While I gasped inwardly at the audacity of the prayer, she added by way of corollary, "And while you're about it, would you please send a dolly for the little girl so she'll know you really love her?"

As often with children's prayers, I was put on the spot. Could I honestly say, "Amen"? I just did not believe that God could do this. Oh, yes, I know that he can do everything. The Bible says so. But there are limits, aren't there? The only way God could answer this particular prayer would be by sending me a parcel from the homeland. I had been in Africa for almost four years and had never, ever received a parcel from home. Anyway, if anyone did send me a parcel, who would put in a hot-water bottle? I lived on the equator!

Halfway through the afternoon, while I was teaching in the nurses' training school, a message was sent that there was a car at my front door. By the time I reached home, the car had gone, but there, on the verandah, was a large, twenty-two pound parcel. I felt tears pricking my eyes. I could not open the parcel alone, so I sent for the orphanage children.

Together we pulled off the string, carefully undoing each knot. We folded the paper, taking care not to tear it unduly. Excitement was mounting. Some thirty or forty pairs of eyes were focused on the large cardboard box.

From the top I lifted out brightly colored, knitted jerseys. Eyes sparkled as I gave them out. Then there were the knitted bandages for the leprosy patients, and the children looked a little bored. Then came a box of mixed raisins and sultanas that would make a nice batch of buns for the weekend. Then, as I put my hand in again, I felt the . . . could it really be? I grasped it and pulled it out. Yes, a brand-new, rubber, hot-water bottle! I cried. I had not asked God to send it; I had not truly believed that he could.

Ruth was in the front row of the children. She rushed forward, crying out, "If God has sent the bottle, he must have sent the dolly, too!" Rummaging down to the bottom of the box, she pulled out the small, beautifully-dressed dolly. Her eyes shone! She had never doubted. Looking up at me, she asked, "Can I go over with you, Mummy, and give this dolly to that little girl so she'll know that God really loves her?"

The parcel had been on the way for five whole months! Packed up by former Sunday school class members whose leader had heard and obeyed God's prompting to send a hot-water bottle, even to the equator. And one of the girls had put in a dolly for an African child . . . five months before in answer to the believing prayer of a ten-year-old girl to bring it "that afternoon."

A Love Note from God

I know what you need before you
even ask me . . . and I will always
give good things to you
when you ask!

—Matthew 6:8, 7:11, adapted

Your Love Note to God

Dear God,

_____

_____

_____

_____

_____

_____

_____

_____

I love you. _____

I never knew up to that time
that God loves us so much.
This heart of mine began
to thaw out;
I could not keep back the tears.
I just drank it in . . .
I tell you there is one thing
that draws
above everything else in the world,
and that is love.

—D. L. Moody

How great is the love
I have for you
as your Father. I will lavish
it on you!
And you will be called my
children.

—1 John 3:1, adapted

CHAPTER SEVEN

I Will Lead
You Home

Five years had passed since the horrible day Bailey had been kidnapped from Uncle Tucker's truck in front of the little corner grocery store. Bailey, now ten, couldn't remember too much about the big house on the Circle B ranch anymore. She could remember her pretty mother and big, happy daddy. Really, she remembered more how warm and safe it felt to be with them than how they looked anymore.

One thing she could remember well, though, was Dusty, her Palomino pony that Uncle Tucker had taught her to ride. How she missed Dusty. She had loved his beautiful blond mane and long, flowing tail. She would giggle when his big lips tickled her hand when she gave him a lump of sugar. And she would laugh when he nuzzled her neck playfully. His big, brown, chocolate-drop eyes followed her adoringly. And he had learned to kneel down on his front knees so her short legs could get into the saddle. They were best friends.

Susan, the woman who had taken her from the pickup that day, wasn't such a bad person really. Bailey had heard her say to herself one time that she had taken Bailey to replace her little girl who died of pneumonia. She was always quiet and sad. So Bailey had just learned to play by herself and not bother Susan as they constantly moved from town to town.

Susan was always looking over her shoulder to see if anybody was watching them or following them. She was really nervous and worried all the time. And if Bailey got out of her sight, even for a second, she panicked.

Bailey thought about the ranch all the time.

She wanted to go home, but she didn't know where the ranch was. She knew her mother's and daddy's names were Wade and Tracy, but she couldn't remember their last name. She had been too little at the time. And Uncle Tucker was just Uncle Tucker. And Dusty? Well, he was a pony; so that didn't help.

One day Bailey was sitting in the waiting area of a beauty shop. Susan was getting her hair cut, while Bailey sat looking through a *National Horseman* magazine. Bailey loved looking at the beautiful horses.

Suddenly she stopped and stared at a picture. Why did the three people look so familiar to her? It was an article about training Palomino horses. She studied the picture more closely, and her eyes grew wide in recognition. Then she read the caption: "Trainer Tucker Jobe with champion stud Dusty Lane and owners Wade and Tracy Walters of the Circle B Ranch in Big Horn, Wyoming."

Bailey got so excited she could hardly stand it. The article showed other photographs of the ranch, too. Home! It was really home!

Then she stopped, dead still. But how could she contact them with Susan watching her every move? *Oh, how I want to go home!* she thought. *I've just got to think of a way to contact them.*

She sat very still, thinking of every possibility. Susan was almost finished with her haircut, and they would be leaving soon. What could she do?

Suddenly Bailey had an idea. She spotted a cell phone lying on one of the hairdressers' work stations near the rest room at the back of the salon. *Yes, it might work, if I'm careful,* she thought.

She closed the magazine and tucked it under her arm, then she walked over to Susan and said, "I'm going to the rest room before we leave."

"All right, honey, but hurry."

As she passed the last station, she picked up the cell phone and ducked into the rest room, locking the door behind her. Quickly she dialed 911 and waited for someone to answer.

"Emergency services," said the voice. "What is your emergency?"

Bailey quickly told her who she was, where she was, and why she was calling. "Please, hurry, before she takes me away again!"

"Stay in the rest room, Bailey, and keep the door locked. Don't open the door for anyone but the police. All right? I'm sending them out to you right now. And don't hang up. Stay on the phone with me until they come."

"All right, but Susan will be really mad. So please hurry."

Suddenly, Bailey jumped when Susan knocked on the rest room door. "Bailey, hurry up, honey. We have to go."

"OK, I'll be out in just a minute," said Bailey nervously.

When another two or three minutes had elapsed, Susan knocked again, this time with more insistence. "Bailey, now you've been in there long enough. Come on, let's go."

"I'm coming. I just need to wash my hands." Then she whispered to the woman on the phone. "What do I do now? She's getting upset."

"Just stay in the rest room with the door locked, Bailey. The police should be there any minute now. Hold on!"

Bailey heard another phone ring in the salon, and one of the hairdressers answered it: "Scissors Palace." Then it was quiet for several seconds.

"All right. I understand. Don't worry. We'll take care of everything."

Susan knocked on the door again. This time she was really angry. "Bailey, get out here! Right now! No more delays. I want to leave."

Then Bailey heard the hairdresser's voice. "She's not going anywhere, lady. And neither are you. Your criminal days are over. We know you kidnapped that little girl, and the police will be here any second now. So just sit down over there and keep quiet."

Susan looked around the room. Three hairdressers were lined up blocking the front door. Two more were at the back door. And now two moved to stand between her and the rest room door just as the police came through the front door. Within minutes they had arrested Susan and taken her away. Meanwhile, Bailey was still locked in the rest room.

Bailey heard a gentle knock on the door. "Bailey, honey, this is Officer Lucas. It's safe, and you can come out now."

Bailey opened the door and peeked out, looking around for Susan.

"Where's Susan?" she asked nervously.

"She's been taken away, Bailey. She will never be able to hurt you or take you away again."

"Oh, thank you. Officer Lucas, can I go home now?"

"Yes, Bailey, you sure can. And I'm going to take you there myself. It's about an hour's drive from here to the Circle B."

It was the longest hour of her life. Finally, though, she saw the familiar white fence that surrounded the ranch. *I'm home!* she thought. *I'm really home.*

As they rounded the last bend in the road and came to the beginning of the white fence, Bailey caught her breath. Standing there, looking over the fence, was a magnificent Palomino stallion. When he saw Bailey, he tossed his beautiful blond mane and whinnied. Then he galloped along the fence, keeping pace with the car as they drove up the long drive to the ranch house.

As the car came to a stop, Wade, Tracy, and Uncle Tucker came running out to meet them. And what followed was the sweetest coming home in the county's history.

After a lot of hugging and tears, Bailey heard the big Palomino whinny loudly, paw the ground, and toss his head to get their attention.

"Uncle Tucker, where's Dusty? I want to see Dusty!"

"That's him, sweetheart," he said pointing at the stallion. "He's not a pony anymore, but he remembers you very well."

"Wow! He's gorgeous! Can I go see him? I've missed him so much."

"Yes, of course, you can. Come on," said Uncle Tucker.

As they opened the gate and entered the corral, Dusty came trotting up to Bailey. She petted his velvet nose and put her arms around his big neck. He nuzzled her neck, and she giggled, just like old times. Then, without any prompting, Dusty slowly knelt down on his front knees so Bailey could get on his back. And they galloped happily around the corral together.

Home! It was so wonderful to be home!

Of all the words
in all the world,
I think "home"
is the nicest one of all.

———————————

—Laura Ingalls Wilder,
Little House on the Prairie

Just Three Words

In the shabby basement of an old house in Atlanta, Georgia, lived a young widow and her little girl. During the Civil War, she had married a young Confederate soldier, against her Yankee father's will, and had moved south with him, to Atlanta. Her wealthy father, angry and hurt at what he considered to be her disloyalty, both to him and the North, told her never to come back again.

The soldier had died bravely during the war, and his death left his wife and child without any support. Alone in Atlanta, Margaret did washing, ironing, and other menial jobs that she could find to help her scrape by and feed little Anna. Their clothes became ragged, and they were both ill from sleeping in the damp, cold basement.

Anna loved to hear her mother's stories about her home in the North. She sat in her mother's lap and listened for hours to descriptions of the big, brick house in Boston, the sprawling shade trees, the beautiful flower gardens, and the wide grassy lawn. She loved to imagine the horses trotting across the meadow, the smell of bread baking in the kitchen, and the soft feel of the four-poster featherbeds. Although Anna had never seen her mother's home, she thought it must be marvelous and secretly hoped that some day they would go there to live.

Margaret often sat looking up wistfully through the narrow basement windows at the blue sky, remembering her mama's smile, laughing with her two sisters, chasing her little brother, and sitting on her father's lap. She missed her family and home so much. But there was nothing she could do. She could never earn enough money to pay the train fare to Boston, no matter how hard she worked. And when she remembered her father's hurt, angry expression when she left, she knew there was little hope of ever seeing her family again.

One day the landlady of the house knocked on the basement door. Anna ran to answer, and the lady handed her a letter. Margaret knew immediately that the broadly scrawled handwriting on the envelope was her father's. With trembling fingers she pulled open the flap. When she pulled out the single-sheet letter, two one-hundred dollar bills fell to the floor. The letter had just three words: "Please come home."

As the old saying goes, "Home is where the heart is." And when we love God with all our hearts, as he so wants us to do, then heaven will, indeed, be our home. God, our Father, pleads for us to come home, from whatever faraway place we may have roamed, just as the parents of a prodigal child so desperately want their child to come home. Don't you hear him calling? Won't you answer with your heart?

A Love Note from God

I will have a house for you—
it will be a home with me
in heaven
that will last forever.
Please come home.

—2 Corinthians 5:1, adapted

Your Love Note to God

Dear God,

_____

_____

_____

_____

_____

_____

_____

_____

_____

I love you. _____

Come home, come home,
You who are weary, come home;
Earnestly, tenderly, Jesus is calling,
Calling, O sinner, come home!

—Will Thompson, 1880